Let's Draw
DOGS AND CATS

by MANNY and ROCHELLE VALDIVIA

Published by McClanahan Book Company, Inc.
23 West 26th Street, New York, NY 10010
Printed in the U.S.A.
ISBN: 0-7681-0222-7

10 9 8 7 6 5 4 3 2 1

SCOTTIE
(SCOTTISH TERRIER)

IN THE SNOW
(SIBERIAN HUSKY)

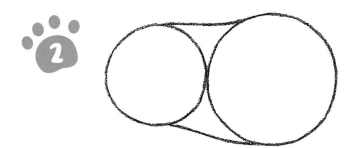

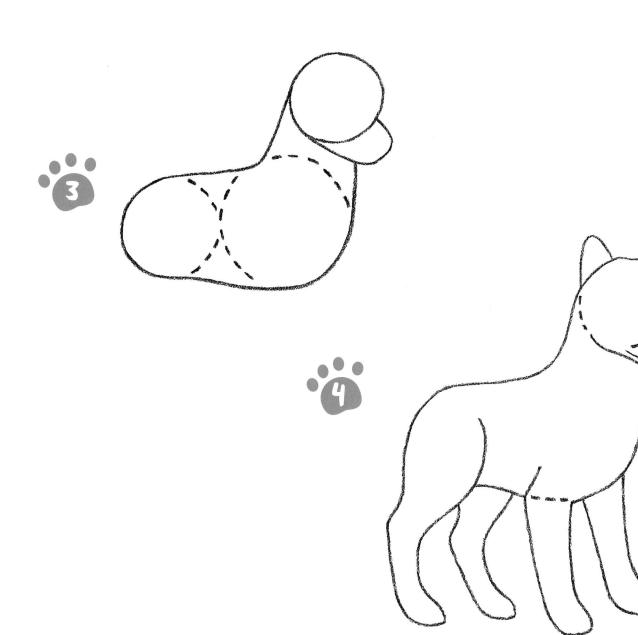

REGAL BEAGLE
(BEAGLE)

Lé POODLE

(POODLE)

ON THE SPOT
(DALMATIAN)

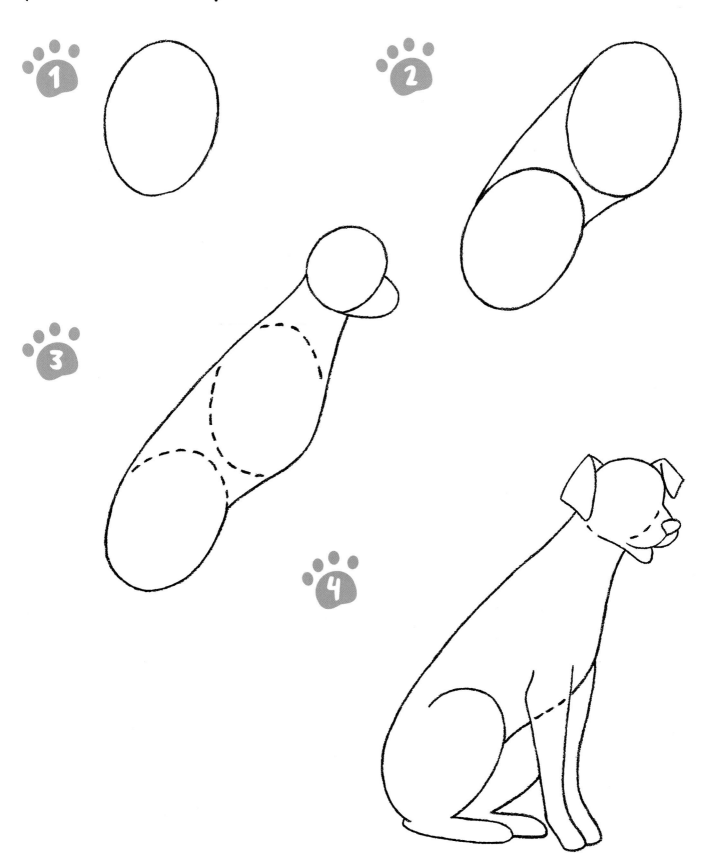

PROUD COLLIE

(COLLIE)

SPEEDY
(GREYHOUND)

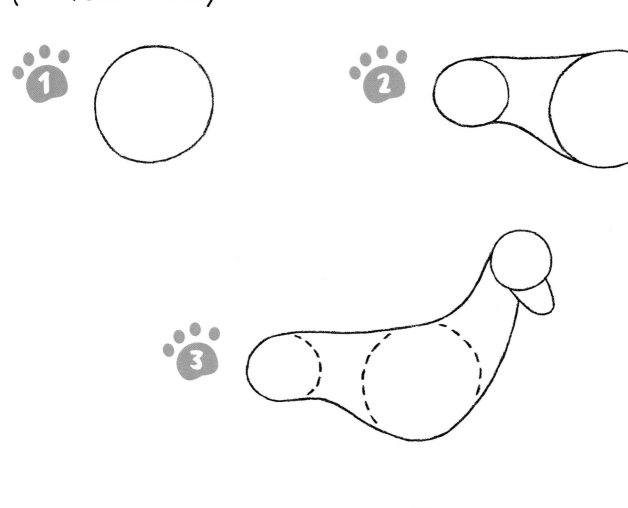

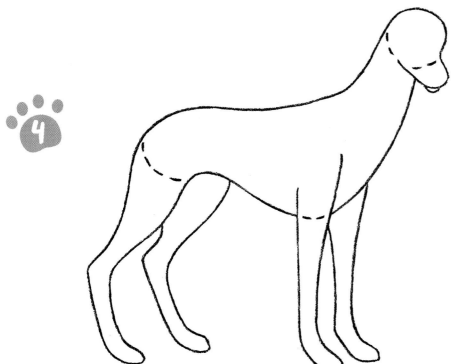

WATCH OUT!
(GERMAN SHEPHERD)

CHOPS
(BULLDOG)

YOU'RE A SAINT

(ST. BERNARD)

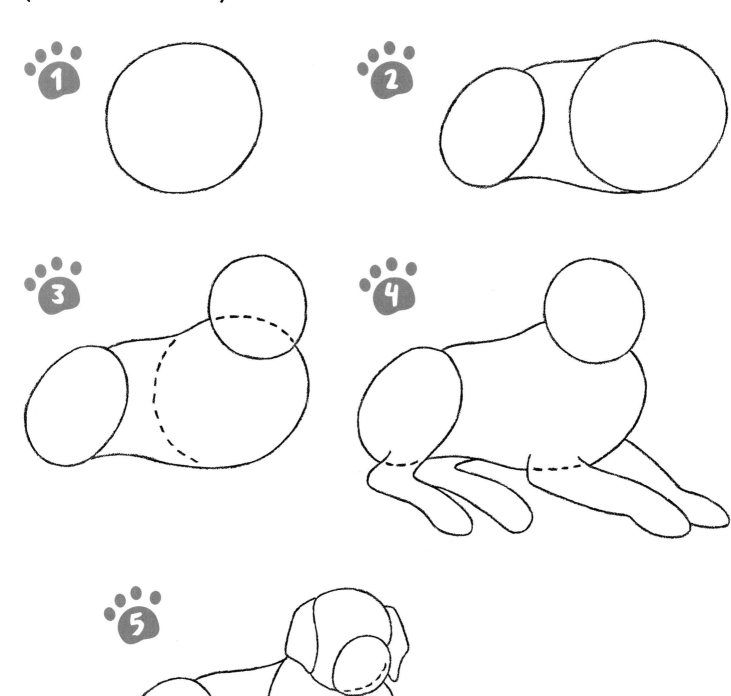

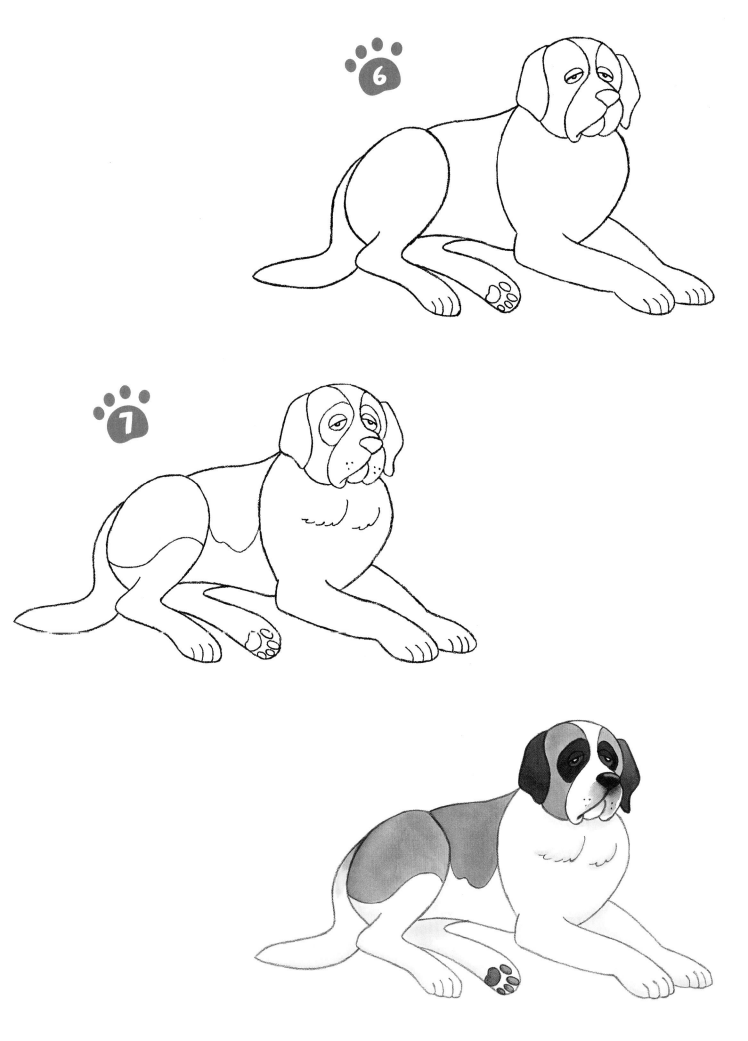

BLACK & WHITE

(BLACK & WHITE NORWEGIAN FOREST)

PUFFY PERSIAN
(ORANGE-EYED WHITE PERSIAN)

COOL CALICO

(CALICO)

CLEVER SIAMESE
(LILAC POINT SIAMESE)

SAVVY TABBY
(BLACK SILVER MACKEREL TABBY)

GOODNITE